The Devil at Midnight

A thriller

Brian Clemens

Samuel French — London
New York - Toronto - Hollywood

CHARACTERS

Elizabeth 'Liz' Burns; 40-something
Nicki White; 26 (although the script could be amended to
   accommodate a younger or older actress)
Jack Burns; nudging 50
Billy; 20-something

Voices only:

Janey; female, young
Clancy; male, sinister
Ian Morton; male, about 60

The action of the play takes place in the living-room of the
Burns' family home

Time — the present

INTERRUPTED SPEECHES

A speech usually follows the one before it BUT:

When one character starts speaking before the other has finished, the point of interruption is marked /. For example:

Jack I don't know. I don't know what I'm thinking. Nobody there. (*He lets the drapes drop back into place*) Is this some kind of visitation? You start digging into Labrador House — and suddenly Martha is dead and we are at each other's throats ... / what is going on ...?

Liz (*interjecting*) Visitation? Something psychic, you mean? The Devil's work?

Other plays by Brian Clemens
published by Samuel French Ltd:

Anybody for Murder? (*with Dennis Spooner*)
Edge of Darkness
Inside Job
Shock!
A Sting in the Tale (*with Dennis Spooner*)
Will You Still Love Me in the Morning? (*with Dennis Spooner*)

ACT I

Scene 1

The living-room of the Burns' family home. Summer. Late afternoon

The house is situated in one of those exclusive "closes" where a few executive-style homes enjoy comparative privacy in the environs of a large town or city. The furnishings are of excellent quality, tasteful, with some genuine antiques — but it has all been well-lived in, so that the general impression is of welcome and comfort

us, a door leads to a hallway and an offstage front door. Nearby a draped window affords a restricted view of the front of the house and the close beyond. R is a door leading off stage to the kitchen and dining areas. L, a staircase leads to the bedrooms. There are shelves containing books, bric-a-brac, and a high-tech phone and answerphone which, at the touch of a button, can be amplified. There are a sofa, some comfortable chairs, a standard lamp and, since the seating area also doubles as "surgery" to a psychoanalyst, a table or desk, looking pretty untidy, with a table lamp, framed photograph, desk diary and papers, etc. on it. Somewhere in the room are a framed diploma and a radio. There is also an area for drinks and glasses

When the Curtain *rises, the radio is playing loud music*

There is a pause, then the phone rings

Elizabeth — "Liz" — Burns enters from the kitchen area. She is an attractive forty-something. She wears an apron and carries a spatula and, for someone who has made a career of sorting out other people's problems, she seems somewhat disorganized. She is torn between the radio and the phone for the briefest moment then quickly moves to snap off the radio and punch the amplifier button on the phone

Liz Elizabeth Burns.
Janey's Voice (*amplified*) Momsie?
Liz Janey! Can you hold on a moment, I'm just sweating some onions. Won't be a moment.

Liz exits into the kitchen area

There is a beat, and then the front doorbell starts to ring

Liz enters from the kitchen area, removing her apron

Liz Oh my God, I have to get some help around here. Janey, someone at the front door, with you in a minute.

Liz exits through the hallway door

Janey's Voice Mom, you don't need help. You give help.
Nicki (*off*) Dr Burns, I'm Nicki White.
Liz (*off*) Yes, of course, come in ——

Liz enters, ushering in Nicki White. Nicki is in her mid-twenties and is very trendily dressed, but not in designer stuff — she doesn't have that kind of money to play with. She is a tough, spunky girl, with today's fashionable power and aggression about her

—— but please bear with me. Sit down, make yourself comfortable.

Nicki doesn't sit down, but just stands there

(*Gesturing to the phone, explaining*) My daughter.
Janey's Voice Mom, if this is a bad time ...
Liz Never. (*She snaps off the phone amplifier, picks up the handset and talks more intimately*) How are you, darling? And how is my favourite grandchild? ... Well, all right, my only grandchild — until November that is. How is Molly? ... Bruises where? She must have done it to herself. I remember, when you were a baby ... (*She glances at Nicki*) You haven't heard from Sam, I suppose? ... No, and I don't expect you will. Yes, your father's fine. ... No, no, onions. ... (*She becomes convulsed with giggles during the following*) Yes, it is a strange term — sweating onions; sounds like you're taking them for a jog — or interrogating them. ... Janey, you're disgusting. I don't know where you get it from. ... Yes, I suppose it must be me. What about this weekend? ... Oh, your father will be disappointed. So will I. But I understand, it's something you have to do. Perhaps next week? ... Call us and let us know. Call us anyway. ... Love you too, darling. Take care. (*She hangs up. To Nicki*) Sorry about that. My daughter Janey. She has an adorable little girl, and another due at the end of the year.

Nicki just stares at Liz

Yes. Nicki White, isn't it? You called me earlier.

Nicki Yes.

Liz Referred to me by Dr Pates. Appointment for 5.30 — (*she rifles through the papers on her desk*) — but I can't find any paperwork, anything that says / I was due to see you.

Nicki (*interjecting*) He definitely said 5.30.

Liz I'm sure he did. Just forgot to tell me, that's all. Freddy Pates is like that: nice man, terrific doctor, but as far as organization goes … Well — put him in a brewery and all the guests would be teetotal.

Nicki Did you try calling him?

Liz Yes. All I got was a recorded message. He's taking a short holiday and his office is closed. Probably off on that boat of his somewhere.

Nicki He said to be here at 5.30.

Liz I believe you, but I have no documents, no case history. So why don't you sit down and tell me about yourself?

Nicki OK. (*She turns to regard the chairs and sofa*) Is this where you tease the demons out?

Liz Demons?

Nicki I dunno … I imagined — you'd have a couch.

Liz Black leather, reclining, me looming over you? Won't the sofa do? Or better still, the chair. We can look at each other eye to eye and you can tell me why Freddy Pates recommended that you come to see me.

Nicki He said you could help me. Said you were the best doctor he knew

Liz I'm not a doctor per se. Plain Mrs. PhD and a diploma to prove it.

Nicki Mrs Burns …

Liz Call me Liz. And please do sit down.

Nicki finally sits in a chair

Liz Right. First let's get some personal details. (*She sits at the desk and writes on a form*) It's Nicki White, yes? Nicki is Nicola?

Nicki I was born on Christmas Day. My dad said I was the best Christmas present he ever had.

Liz That immediately tells me something: you were wanted — welcomed — and your father loved you.

Nicki (*suddenly impassioned*) You don't know how much!

Liz is a bit taken aback by this sudden show of passion, but carries on calmly

Liz How about your parents?

Nicki They're both dead. I never really knew my mother, she died when I was a baby. Dad brought us up.

Liz Us? So you have other family?

Nicki Just my brother, Billy.

Liz How old are you, Nicki?

Nicki Twenty-six in December.

Liz (*writing*) December 25th, right? Are you, or have you been, married?

Nicki No.

Liz Other close relationships? A boyfriend ...?

Nicki Just my brother, Billy.

Liz Are you very close?

Nicki He'd do anything for me. Anything at all.

Liz Current address?

Nicki We have a room at 22, Barley Road.

Liz We? You and your brother? Not two rooms?

Nicki Just a room.

Liz Are you currently employed?

Nicki I was. Billy works for a phone company; he got me a job in the office, but I had to give it up.

Liz Why?

Nicki I couldn't cope.

Liz Why couldn't you cope?

Nicki That's why I'm here, isn't it? Why Dr Pates sent me to you. (*She sniffs*) What's that smell?

Liz Damn! My onions. Excuse me.

Liz rushes off into the kitchen

Nicki looks around. She sees the framed photo on the desk, picks it up and studies it

Liz enters from the kitchen

So much for Cordon Bleu. The can opener will be red hot tonight! (*She sees that Nicki is studying the photo*)

Nicki Is this your daughter?

Liz Yes.

Nicki And this is her daughter — right?

Liz (*nodding*) Molly. Isn't she beautiful?

Nicki Yeah. Nice-looking kid. So — vulnerable.

Liz Vulnerable?

Nicki Make sure you take good care of her.

Liz We do. She's a happy, healthy little girl with a mother who dotes on her, and grandparents who / love her to bits.

Nicki (*interjecting*) Who would go through hell and back to protect her?

Liz (*taken aback*) I'm an agnostic. I don't share the concept that hell exists.

Nicki It does. I promise you it does.

Liz Nicki, I know it's not your fault, but this consultation wasn't on my agenda. I can spare you a little time, but I'm afraid / it won't be too long.

Nicki (*interjecting, indicating the photo*) You didn't mention a father. "A mother who dotes on her", but you didn't mention Molly's father. He around? Or did he run off — leave her all alone?

Liz We're here to talk about you.

Nicki But fathers are important, aren't they? What they do, or don't do?

Liz (*anxious to restore her ascendancy*) Tell me about your father.

Nicki I already told you, my dad's dead.

Liz Was it because of him that Freddy Pates sent you to me?

Nicki clams up

I can't help you unless I know what's troubling you.

Nicki I'm having trouble sleeping.

Liz Did Dr Pates give you a physical check-up?

Nicki Yes.

Liz And?

Nicki I'm fine. So it's gotta be something mental — right? Something in my mind?

Liz Insomnia can be the symptom of something deeper, yes. How long have you had trouble sleeping?

Nicki I used to go months, years even, without having them.

Liz Having what?

Nicki The nightmares. Now they come every night, even if I take a pill — they come, and I wake up screaming, at midnight, always midnight.

Liz Why midnight? Do you know?

Nicki That's when it must have happened to me. That's what Dr Pates reckoned.

Liz When what happened?

Nicki I don't really know — it's all so hazy … That's why I came to you.

Liz Every night at midnight?

Nicki On the dot.

Liz What if you stay up late — after midnight?

Nicki I've tried that. The next night it's even worse, more terrifying — as though he's punishing me.

Liz Who's punishing you?

Nicki The Devil.

Liz The Devil? Why the Devil?

Nicki Because I see him. This close. I'm going crazy — aren't I?

Liz Crazy isn't in my vocabulary. Disturbed, certainly. Is it always the same nightmare?

Nicki Always.

Liz Can you recount it for me?

Nicki It's all mixed up.

Liz Try. Tell me what this "devil" does.

Nicki He embraces me. Lifts me from my bed. Then he holds me close; I can smell the garlic on his breath, along with the stale stink of tobacco. His beard scratches my face. He has a pointy little beard.

Liz And horns and tail?

Nicki You don't believe me, do you?

Liz I believe that what you see in your dream is real to you.

Nicki coughs

Would you like some water?

Nicki Thanks. This thing is running me down. I think I may be getting a cold.

Liz moves to the drinks table, opens a small bottle of mineral water, pours some into a glass and gives it to Nicki during the following

Liz After he lifts you from your bed and holds you close — what happens after that?

Nicki I think he just takes me away. I get the impression of a journey.

Liz Where does he take you?

Nicki I don't know. It's bright, very bright, then it's dark again. There's a big house, by the sea.

Liz Can you see the sea?

Nicki No. But I can hear it. Waves breaking on the rocks far below.

Liz This house is high up then? On a cliff?

Nicki I suppose so. I never see it clearly. The impression is — of cold ... I'm very cold, and this big, grey house. Bright, dark — it's a light that keeps coming on and off. No, it keeps coming around! Bright, dark, bright, dark. A lighthouse! Way off somewhere, lighting up the big gates. That's something, isn't it — I never remembered the gates before! (*She becomes more excited*) There's a name. I remember a name — above the gates.

Liz Concentrate on that. The name above the gates — do you know what it says?

Nicki It might be — a dogs' home. It has something to do with dogs. Or a dog. Yes, a big, black dog like our neighbours used to have. A labrador! That's it — definitely a labrador. Are we getting anywhere?

Liz You're doing well, Nicki. Can you remember what happens next — after you arrive at the house?

Nicki He takes me inside. I can smell his breath again — garlic and tobacco. There are other people around — I think. He puts me down on a bed. (*She* *pauses*) That's when I wake up shaking, in a cold sweat — screaming inside. It's all I can recall. Can you help me?

Liz What happens when you wake up?

Nicki Usually I find Billy, grab him, hold him close.

Liz Is Billy in your nightmare?

Nicki No. Yes. He's in it somewhere, but I don't think I see him. But he is there.

Liz What does he think about these nightmares?

Nicki Billy doesn't think. He just holds me tight until I stop shaking.

Liz Until eventually you go back to sleep again?

Nicki No. Not properly. I lie in his arms and I watch the window, waiting for the light to come. I'm so tired. What's wrong with me?

Liz Dr Pates was right, your insomnia is the symptom of some earlier trauma.

Nicki Something bad that happened to me?

Liz Yes.

Nicki Then why can't I remember it?

Liz You don't want to, it's too painful. So your brain is blotting it out, concealing it behind this fiction of devils and demons.

Nicki But it seems so real.

Liz Dreams always do at the time, but does it seem feasible now you're awake?

Nicki No. But there is something there.

Liz I agree, and we'll "tease it out", eh? Together?

Nicki Do you know, I feel a bit better, I think I might sleep tonight.

Liz Because you're sharing it now. Would you like some more water?

Nicki Please.

Liz (*pouring another glass of water*) You're sure this dog is a labrador?

Nicki Yes.

Liz And, in your mind, it's associated with the house on the cliff?

Nicki It must be. Why else would I mention it?

Liz hands Nicki the glass. Nicki drinks

Liz Does he lift you easily from your bed?

Nicki Yes.

Liz You must be light then. Young.

Nicki (*matter-of-factly*) I am seven years old. (*Startled*) How did I know that?

Liz (*tapping Nicki's head*) It's all in there, Nicki. Waiting to spill out. Does the Devil have a face?

Nicki I told you, a pointy beard, foul breath ...

Liz But does he remind you of someone you know — or knew? Your father, a close relative — a friend?

Nicki The Devil? (*She pauses*) It's a face I will never forget. Never.
Liz That's enough for now. (*She rifles through her desk diary*) I want to see
  you again soon. Can you make tomorrow at 4.30?
Nicki Yes.
Liz 4.30 it is then.
Nicki You will help me?
Liz That's why you're here. Now I want you to go home and get a good
  night's sleep. (*She opens the door into the hallway*)

*Jack Burns is framed in the doorway. He is a slim, clean-shaven man
knocking fifty, but still virile, sexy even. He wears a casual jacket and
carries a couple of squash racquets*

*Liz, Nicki and Jack are all startled. Nicki, inches from Jack, screams in shock.
Or recognition?*

CURTAIN

SCENE 2

The same, later that night

The drapes are closed

The stage is empty for a moment

Jack enters from the kitchen and pours himself a whisky

Jack Super meal.

  Liz enters from the kitchen

Liz Courtesy of Tesco's and Mr Heinz.
Jack I thought so.
Liz You just said it was super.
Jack It was, but not quite enough garlic for my taste. Want a Scotch?

Liz shakes her head. Jack flops into a chair

Liz I thought you were going to watch cricket.
Jack So did I, but it's raining in Jamaica. Can you imagine, Jamaica, the
  Sunshine Isle? And there's no cricket.

Liz Perhaps there is a God after all.

Jack You're a bit scratchy tonight, aren't you? I said I was sorry for barging in on your consultation. Wasn't expecting you to be having one; you don't much these days, not since you got all that hospital work.

Liz Sinecures that you arranged.

Jack Don't knock it. As County Controller I have a lot of clout, and I don't see why I shouldn't use it in the family interests. Anyway, it isn't nepotism, not really — you were definitely the best person for the job. (*He drains his glass, gets up and pours another*)

Liz You're drinking a lot tonight.

Jack You are scratchy. What is it? That girl get under your skin? Who is she?

Liz Her name is Nicola White.

Jack And what's her problem?

Liz You know I never discuss cases with you or anyone. Client confidentiality. I have ethics.

Jack Meaning I don't? You know that's not true. What's got into you, Liz?

Liz moves over to the whisky

Liz I will have one.

Jack Now who's drinking a lot? Anyway — I have a reason to celebrate.

Liz regards Jack

It's still under wraps — nothing's settled — but Ian Morton dropped by today.

Liz The MP?

Jack It won't be announced for weeks yet. Morton is retiring, stepping down before the next election, and they want to start grooming a new candidate now.

Liz You?

Jack It's on the cards. The Honourable Member for. What do you think?

Liz I ... I don't know what to think.

Jack Come on, we've discussed the possibility before, and you agreed I'd be right for it. Aren't you pleased for me?

Liz Of course I'm pleased.

Jack Let me tell Janey. When she comes this weekend let me / tell her the good news.

Liz (*interjecting*) Janey isn't coming. She wants to catch up on that business course.

Jack Some damned course before family?

Liz Face facts. She hasn't heard from Sam in weeks, and she's not going to. You ask me, he's gone back to Australia, and she's on her own with a young

child and another on the way. She's resigned to making her own way alone
— and I agree with her.

Jack I wish she'd move nearer us.

Liz She wants her independence, Jack.

Jack But sitting in that cottage in the middle of nowhere … Dammit, she
needs a man.

Liz Maybe she's better off without one.

Jack Oh, we're anti-male now, are we?

Liz I'm thinking of what's best for Janey. If she passes this course she could
get a good job, one that pays enough for a child-minder. But I agree with
you. I wish she would move a little nearer.

Jack I was looking forward to them coming. The weekend won't be the same
without Janey — and little Molly. I just love that kid to bits, you know that?

Liz So you should, she's your grand-daughter.

Jack D'you know what gives me the biggest kick? Last thing at night, when
I slip into her room and just look at her. So — innocent … I want to throw
a shield around her, protect her.

Liz Protect her from what?

Jack Growing up. Life. Oh well, they will come down next weekend?

Liz Probably. Would you like coffee?

Jack Later maybe. I'll nurse this (*the whisky*) — for a while.

Liz Jack, didn't you once work in a place called Labrador House?

Jack Don't remind me. It was the year before we met. I was only there a few
months, but that was enough.

Liz It was by the sea, wasn't it?

Jack The sea? The tempest! It stood atop of the Scottish headland with waves
crashing below; whole time I was there, I never remember a calm day.

Liz What was it like — as a building I mean?

Jack Are you doing a thesis on Victorian follies?

Liz Humour me.

Jack Labrador House could have been a role model for Bleak House. Grim,
grey — built by some mad Canadian millionaire back in the 1880s. You
know what I remember most about it? Mice, the smell of mice. We tried
every means known to man, but we never could get rid of them. Mice have
no sphincter muscle, did you know that? Whenever they move, wherever
they go, they wee. It was years before I got that sweet, musky, foul smell
out of my nostrils. They pulled the place down nearly twenty years ago,
thank God. I like to think the mice did a lemming and threw themselves off
the cliff when their home was gone.

Liz What about the lighthouse? There was a lighthouse?

Jack Was, and still is. Used to keep me awake at nights. The light coming
and going.

Liz Bright, dark, bright dark.

Jack Liz, what is this all about?

Liz What did they use the house for?

Jack It was a kind of half-way house.

Liz For whom?

Jack Children in need of care.

Liz Abused children?

Jack Some. Most of the kids were moved on within days, others stayed for weeks. This is not my idea of a celebration!

Liz Was there a large staff?

Jack Is there ever? At any one time, twenty to twenty-five social workers, carers, nurses — the budget wouldn't run to more. What brought this on? Did you read about Martha Myers in the papers?

Liz Who's Martha Myers?

Jack She was at the house for a while — she's over here on a lecture tour.

Liz Martha Myers? Isn't she some kind of American quack?

Jack There was a time when we believed in her theories. Some still do.

Liz I remember her now, a disciple of perceived memory and denial. If you ask the patient, "Did your family abuse you?" and they say "No", they really mean "Yes" and are in denial. What was she doing at the house?

Jack I've had enough of this.

Liz Jack, I promise you it's important to me. Could be important.

Jack All right. It was at the time of that *cause célèbre* in the Scottish Islands. Martha was our psychological advisor.

Liz "*Cause célèbre*"?

Jack Accusations of satanic abuse.

Jack's words hang in the air for a moment

Liz Who was principal at the time?

Jack Liz / ...

Liz (*overriding*) Who?

Jack Paul Stevens.

Liz Our Paul?

Jack Our Paul, who's fancied you for yonks and sat in that chair a hundred times.

Liz Did he have a beard then?

Jack A beard?

Liz Did he?

Jack A beard? I don't know. In those days we all of us sported a beard at one time or another.

Liz All? You too?

Jack It was *de rigeur* amongst young social workers then; pints in straight glasses, plebeian poets and beards. Did I have a beard? I had a muff! All around, then I decided I looked like a demented ferret peering through a hedge so I trimmed it down to a neat and elegant goatee ... Used to stroke it like so, (*he demonstrates*) while I puffed on my pipe and pontificated.

Liz You smoked? I didn't know you ever smoked.

Jack OK, you have me, you've broken me down, I confess. I once puffed on a pipe. Thought it gave me authority. Matter of fact I got hooked on the deadly weed for a while, graduated to fags, twenty a day — took me nearly a year to quit. Is that it? Have you delved deep enough into my mis-spent youth? What say we now investigate your flirtations with hash and Thai-grass and dancing barefoot and bare-arsed and God knows what else at Glastonbury or wherever?

Liz I need a top-up. (*She tops up her glass during the following*)

Jack moves to Liz

Were there big gates at the house. With the name above them?

Jack No! That's enough, I'm not continuing this conversation. For God's sake, Liz, despite the lack of garlic, I had a great dinner. I had great news to tell you — why are you behaving like this? I love you, Liz.

Liz And I love you.

Jack Well, then. (*He embraces her*) It was that girl, wasn't it? Nicola Whatshername?

Liz Why do you say that?

Jack Deduction. Elementary, my dear Elizabeth. I arrive. She leaves. Having screamed at me as though I were the Devil himself, and suddenly you're all steamed up and / acting strangely ...

Liz (*interjecting*) The Devil? Why the Devil?

Jack Why not? Just a figure of speech. What would you prefer, the dogs of war, the four horsemen of the Apocalypse? Liz. Liz?

Liz I'm sorry. I was being stupid. Letting my imagination run wild. (*She caresses his face*) I was mad to even think ... You could never harm anyone, could you?

Jack I think you've had one drink too many. Have I been neglecting you?

Liz No.

Jack Yes, I have. Off chasing my own ambitions. You need a holiday. We both need a holiday. What about Freddy Pates? The times he's offered us that boat of his.

Liz Freddy's away.

Jack If he was, he's back. I saw him in town this morning.

Liz Freddy? It couldn't have been.

Jack If it wasn't him it was his double — driving his car.

Liz But I called his office this afternoon and was told he was away.

Jack Who told you?

Liz Some anonymous female.

Jack Answerphone?

Liz Yes.

Jack That explains all — we know all about Freddy's organizational skills. He forgot to erase the message. Anyway, forget Freddy, we don't need him. We'll go under our own steam … Barbados — Jamaica.

Liz It's raining in Jamaica.

Jack Then we'll take umbrellas. And galoshes. And spend a lot of time indoors — just the two of us, eh? It's been a long time since we did that.

Liz We can't go before Janey has her baby.

Jack Why not? It's three months off, she's fit, healthy and, as you keep pointing out, independent. Say yes, Liz.

Liz All right. When?

Jack Any time after tomorrow night. We've got that Chamber of Commerce dinner.

Liz I could easily forego that collection of stuffed shirts.

Jack Influential people, that's what they are, and Ian Morton will be there. Along with his agent and chairman of committee. Let's not forget the main prize.

Liz Very well. The end of the month then.

Jack I'll get Patsy on to it soon as I get to the office. I think I'd like that coffee now, do you want me to / get it?

Liz (*interjecting*) I'll do it.

Jack Then perhaps we could have a rehearsal for the holiday, eh? An early night? I'm told that success is sexy.

Liz You're not there yet.

Jack Come to bed, I'll give you a preview of the honourable member.

Jack kisses Liz. She responds. They hold close for a moment, then she breaks away. There is a pause

Liz You're incorrigible. But you do look kind of sexy. And, for the record, I didn't go bare-arsed. I'm a nice girl, I am. Just bare boobs.

Jack And a fine and wondrous sight it was, I'm sure.

Liz Do you want de-caff?

Jack No. If we're going to bed early I want to stay awake. I don't want to miss anything!

Liz Don't go away.

Liz exits into the kitchen

Jack happily prowls away towards the drinks. He finishes his whisky and notices the bottle

Jack What the hell. (*He pours himself another, then prowls back to the desk, idly touches the papers, then picks up the form Liz filled in about Nicki and starts to read*)

The doorbell rings

Jack is mildly surprised. He looks at his watch, then exits into the hallway

We hear Nicki's and Jack's voices indistinctly, then;

Nicki (*off*) Out of my way!
Jack (*off*) Wait a minute …

Nicki enters from the hallway in a rush. She is distraught and tousled, hugging a roughly wrapped package to herself. During the following she is breathless and panting

Jack enters behind her

Jack Do you know what time it is?
Nicki I have to see her.
Jack There's a time and place / for everything. (*He makes to touch Nicki*)
Nicki (*pulling away; interjecting*) Don't touch me!

Liz enters from the kitchen

Liz Nicki!
Nicki Mrs Burns. Liz.

Liz hurries to Nicki and embraces her protectively

I tried to sleep, I really did, but then I felt the dreams coming and I got scared … I didn't know what to do. I'm so sorry. I didn't want to barge in like this, but I had to see you. You'll help me, won't you?
Liz Yes, I'll help you. (*She looks beyond Nicki to Jack*)
Jack Liz, this isn't right. There is a time and place.
Liz Jack, why don't you take your drink into the study, and watch some TV?

Jack hesitates, then capitulates and heads towards the kitchen door

Jack This isn't right.
Liz Close the door.

Jack exits, closing the door

Liz steers Nicki to an armchair

Liz Sit down, and calm down.

Nicki sits, clutching the package to her, her aggressive confidence of the previous scene now gone

Seeing you at this time of night is very unprofessional, Nicki. Dammit, so is this. (*She pours a glass of brandy and proffers it to Nicki*) It's brandy. Drink it.

Nicki takes the brandy and sips at it

All of it.

Nicki finishes the glass, coughing on the spirit

I want you to relax — breathe with me. (*She audibly takes deep breaths, gesturing at Nicki*)

Nicki follows Liz's rhythm of breathing

That's better. Sit back, make yourself comfortable. Do you want me to take that …? (*She makes to take the package*)

Nicki hugs the package to her even more tightly

All right, that's OK … You hold on to it.
Nicki I'm sorry — shouldn't have / barged in …
Liz (*interjecting*) Try to understand, Nicki, you don't have to say you're sorry. You're the victim here.

Nicki looks much calmer

That's better. Do you know what the time is? It's 10.50. Not midnight. More than an hour to midnight. Nothing to fear for more than an hour. In fact there's nothing to fear at all. I want you to grasp that thought, hold on to it. You trust me, don't you?
Nicki Yes.
Liz Because I'm your friend. I'm going to help you. Say it.
Nicki You're my friend, you're going to help me.

Liz Good. Wait here a moment.

Liz exits to the kitchen

Nicki waits for a moment, then is impelled to get up and look out of the window

Liz enters carrying a smallish chiming clock. She puts it down and opens the face glass so that the hands can be moved

Are you happy there? Sit wherever you want, wherever you feel at ease.

Nicki sits in the chair. Liz turns some of the lights off so that Nicki and the sofa are more intimately, atmospherically lit

It's time we got down to the nitty gritty. Time to face up. I want to take you through your nightmare again, Nicki.

Nicki stirs, agitated

(*Gripping Nicki's hand*) But not alone. This time I will be with you, every step of the way. Are you up to that?
Nicki You'll be with me? You won't leave me?
Liz I won't leave you.
Nicki All right.
Liz Good girl. Lean back, let the chair embrace you, make yourself really comfortable ... Relax. Relax.

Nicki complies, but still clutches the package

You sure you don't want me to ...? (*She makes to relieve Nicki of her parcel*)

Nicki clutches the parcel even more tightly

Very well. Breathe with me again; long, slow breaths. (*Again, she breathes audibly — slow, long breaths*)

Nicki complies

Close your eyes, Nicki. You are very relaxed ... I suggest you are at peace; you feel as though you are floating — and so calm — so calm, do you feel calm now?
Nicki Yes.

Liz Good — now I want you to count backwards from 10 to 1. Will you do that? 10 to 1.

Nicki 10, 9, 8, 7, 6, 5 … (*She goes into a hypnotic trance and stops counting. Her eyes remain closed during the following*)

Liz Can you hear me?

Nicki Yes.

During the following, Nicki "becomes" the child

Liz What is your name?

Nicki Nicola White. Everyone calls me Nicki.

Liz I want you to go back, Nicki — back to when you were just a little girl, when something bad happened to you. Do you remember that day?

Nicki Yes.

Liz How old are you?

Nicki I'm seven years old.

Liz That's when that bad, bad thing happened to you, didn't it?

Nicki Yes.

Liz At midnight? Did it happen at midnight?

Nicki Yes, yes. (*She becomes agitated*)

Liz (*quickly touching Nicki*) It's not midnight yet, Nicki. No, it's before midnight — do you remember what happened before midnight?

Nicki (*calming down again*) Daddy put me to bed.

Liz What else did Daddy do?

Nicki He kissed me.

Liz Is his face all rough and scratchy?

Nicki Daddy's smooth. He smells nice. Like Uncle Ted.

Liz Is your Uncle Ted there too?

Nicki Oh, yes.

Liz Did he kiss you too?

Nicki No, I kissed him. He's cuddly.

Liz Does he have a beard?

Nicki Uncle Ted? (*She is convulsed with a child's fit of giggles, then subsides into utter stillness*)

Liz What's happening now?

Nicki I'm asleep, silly.

Liz turns the hands of the clock to twelve, and it starts to strike out the hours

Liz Nicki, d'you hear that? 8-9-10-11-12. It's midnight.

Nicki becomes agitated, moving and moaning softly in fear, her eyes closed

Where are you?

Nicki In my bed. I can hear him hurting my daddy. Why is he hurting my daddy? (*A child's cry, wrenched from the heart*) Don't hurt my daddy!

Liz Who is hurting your daddy?

Nicki That man. The Devil, it's the Devil. Make him stop, please make him stop ... No, don't touch me, don't touch me.

Liz Is he with you now?

Nicki He's picking me up, taking me from my bed. I want my daddy. I want to scream ... mmmmmmmmm — he won't let me scream, I can't breathe, he's holding me so tight — his beard's hurting me. I want my daddy! I want Uncle Ted. He won't let him come with me ... Please let Uncle Ted come with me. Please — (*she makes a sound as if gagged*) mmmmmmmmmmmmm. (*She weeps, her chest heaving, sobs being torn out of her*)

Liz (*gripping Nicki's hand*) Take my hand. Hold tight. I'm still here, right with you. Can you hear me, Nicki?

Nicki Yes.

Liz Tell me where you are now. Take your time; where has he taken you?

Nicki To the big house. It's so cold, and the light hurts my eyes. Bright, dark, bright, dark. They're undressing me, they shouldn't do that.

Liz Is there more than one person in the room?

Nicki gets agitated

Nicki, who else is there?

Nicki That woman.

Liz Who is she? What does she look like?

Nicki She's fat, and ugly. Like blubber. She's cross with me.

Liz What is she doing?

Nicki Holding me down.

During the following, Liz becomes caught up in the reconstruction, and finds it hard to distance herself from her own emotions

He's touching me. The Devil's touching me. I want my daddy!

Liz Nicki, does the Devil have a name?

Nicki They're laughing. I can hear them outside the door — laughing.

During the following, the kitchen door gently opens and Jack appears in the doorway

Nicki She's talking to him ... She calls him — something.

Liz Yes, Nicki, what does she call him? What is his name?

Jack Liz.

Nicki sits right up, eyes open. Liz reacts to Nicki's distress and turns to Jack, then hurries over to him. Nicki hunches into herself, rocking gently

Liz Damn you.
Jack I heard the ruckus and I / was worried.
Liz (*overriding*) Get out. Get out!

Liz hustles Jack away into the kitchen

Liz slams the door on Jack, gathers herself, and returns to Nicki

Nicki.

Nicki slowly raises her head

Nicki You promised you wouldn't leave me.
Liz I haven't, I'm right here. With you now.
Nicki Uncle Ted would never leave me. (*She lets the paper slip from her package to reveal it contains a moth-eaten, battered teddy bear. She hugs the bear close to her*) Not Uncle Ted.
Liz You said this woman spoke to the Devil, called him by name ...What was that name?
Nicki (*hugging the bear*) Never leave me, never, never, never. (*She subsides into immobility again*)
Liz Where are you now?
Nicki In bed.
Liz Asleep?
Nicki Drifting.
Liz Are you alone?
Nicki No. The mice are there. Lots of mice.

The phone rings. Liz quickly pushes a button so that the message is recorded on the answerphone, then returns to Nicki. The answerphone light blinks from now on

Liz I am going to count from 10 to 1 now — but when I reach 5, you will wake up. 10, 9, 8, 7, 6 ... 5.

Nicki wakes instantly, a bit dazed. Liz restores the main lights, then moves close to Nicki and strokes the teddy bear

I know who Uncle Ted is now.
Nicki I've had him since I can remember; I take him to bed every night, even

now. Except ... I think there was one time he wasn't with me — someone took him away! Or did they? I'm not sure of anything. What happened?
Liz You took the first step. A big step.
Nicki Did you learn anything?
Liz Someone put you through an ordeal no child should go through.
Nicki Have you found out who?
Liz No. But I will.

Nicki stands up and sways. Liz supports her

Nicki I'm tired.
Liz You can't go home tonight, you'll have to stay here.
Nicki Oh, but I / couldn't do that.
Liz (*interjecting*) I want you to stay.
Nicki I am very tired. I want to sleep.
Liz Yes, you will sleep now.

They exit up the stairs, Liz supporting Nicki

There is a pause, then a tap at the kitchen door

The door opens and Jack enters. He prowls around the room and looks at the recently vacated chair, then at the clock. He closes the face glass on the clock

Liz enters down the stairs

That was a damned fool thing you did — busting in.
Jack I'm sorry. I was concerned — that girl has a mad look in her eye.
Liz That girl is in distress. I've put her in the spare room.

Jack regards Liz

I couldn't load her into a cab, not in the condition she's in.
Jack What condition is that?
Liz Hurt, confused.
Jack That could describe me right now. Well, she certainly ruined our plans for this evening, didn't she? (*He raises his hands placatingly, as if anticipating a protest from Liz*) All right, all right, a soul in pain, you have to respond, I understand that. I think. Are you coming to bed?
Liz In a while.

Jack nods and heads for the stairs, then pauses

Jack Is Jamaica still on?

Liz stares blankly at Jack

   Our holiday in the sun — or the rain, depending on the weather.
Liz Oh, yes.
Jack Well, is it?
Liz Why not.

Jack heads up the stairs

Jack I hope you know what you're doing.

   Jack exits up the stairs

Liz So do I.

Liz remains still for a moment, then sees the blinking light of the answerphone. She switches on the answerphone

   During the playback, Nicki enters on the stairs, and remains at the top of them, gazing down

Janey's Voice (*amplified*) Momsie, Dad. Sorry to call at this time, but I know you're both late birds. I just thought I'd let you know that plans have changed. I can come over with Molly this weekend. Let me know. Love you, 'bye.

Liz snaps off the answerphone, senses something and turns to see Nicki

Nicki You asked me about a name, didn't you? And suddenly it came to me: what they called him. Jack. Jack the Lad.
Liz Are you quite sure about that?
Nicki Yes.
Liz Go back to bed.

   Nicki nods, yawns, and exits

Liz remains still a moment, then comes to a decision, picks up the phone and dials out

Liz (*after a long pause*) Janey? … Yes. … I know what time it is, sorry if I woke you, but I just got your call about this weekend. I'm sorry, darling,

but it won't be convenient for you to come over. We've made other plans.
Yes, darling … Janey, you said earlier that Molly had some bruises …
You're quite sure she did it to herself? I just wondered if … when your
father was playing with her — he can be very rough. … No, darling, I'm
not getting paranoid. … Yes, you go back to sleep, darling … I'll call you
again soon. (*She hangs up. She moves to the foot of the stairs and looks up
them*) Jack the Lad.

CURTAIN

SCENE 3

The same. The following morning

Nicki enters down the stairs, fully dressed and holding her teddy bear

*There is something furtive about her during the following. She looks back up
the stairs, listens, looks around, puts the bear on the sofa and moves gently
to the kitchen door. She opens the door, looks into the room, listening, then
quickly exits into the kitchen*

There is a pause

*Jack enters down the stairs, dressed and ready for work. He glances at his
watch, hurries to the front window, pulls the drapes and looks out. He smiles
and taps on the window*

Jack (*calling off to someone*) Hey! (*He ducks down out of sight, bobs up
again then down again — and then he notices the teddy bear. He picks up
the bear and lifts it up and down, in and out of sight, playing some game
with whoever is beyond the window*)

*During this game, Nicki enters from the kitchen and stops, a bit taken aback
to see Jack*

(*Standing up in full view, wagging the bear's arm to say "goodbye"*) Bye!
Nicki What are you doing with that?

Jack turns to see her, suddenly feeling a bit ridiculous holding the bear

Jack Oh … er …
Nicki Give it me. (*She snatches the bear from Jack, moves to the window and
looks out*)

We hear a car door slam, then a car starting up and driving away

What were you doing?

Jack The kids across the close — off to school ... It's a silly ritual we have.

Nicki Two little girls.

Jack Yeah, they're at that wonderful Alice in Wonderland age, when they are neither woman or child. That's an old man's view — these days they are out of nappies and into dating without ever experiencing that —"in between" when they are still naïve, innocent ...

Nicki Trusting?

Jack (*regarding Nicki*) It's Nicki White, isn't it? We haven't really met. I'm Jack Burns.

Nicki I know.

Jack Did you sleep well?

Nicki As a matter of fact, yes.

Jack Would you like some breakfast?

Nicki I already made myself some coffee. That was all right, wasn't it?

Jack Make yourself at home. Liz is still in the shower, down in a minute I expect. Do I know you? The way you stare at me, I feel you know me.

Nicki There's still some coffee left — if you want some.

Jack I take mine at the office, with a big, sticky bun. It's my first and only pleasure of the day. A beautiful pause before the madness starts.

Nicki Madness?

Jack After ten the phones hardly stop ringing. You're staring again; are you sure we haven't met before? Liz will be down in a moment. She said something about driving you home, but if you're in a hurry I'm leaving in a moment — I could give you a lift.

Nicki No! I'll wait for Liz. We have to arrange for her to see me again.

Jack Yes, of course. She can't be at your beck and call all the time, you know. My wife needs a holiday. We've been planning it for some time; you wouldn't want to disrupt those plans, would you?

Nicki That's up to her.

Jack No, it's up to you. Won't this thing, whatever it is, keep? Can't it be put on the back burner? You like Liz, don't you?

Nicki Yes, I do.

Jack So do I. I love her. She's been working too hard and too long. You could help. Wouldn't you like to help her?

Nicki Yes.

Jack I knew you'd understand, Nicki. You don't mind if I call you Nicki? (*He moves nearer to her*)

Nicki hugs her bear tighter

Is that your security blanket? Surely you're too adult for that? You're not a child any more, are you, Nicki? You're not naïve and innocent any more. (*He makes to touch the bear*)

Nicki hugs the bear closer

Make sure you always carry it in front of you. Or else everyone will see your bare behind! (*He chuckles and makes to touch the bear again*)
Nicki (*pulling back*) Don't touch!

Liz enters down the stairs, wearing a robe

Jack looks at her, feeling inexplicably guilty

Jack It was just a joke. We were talking. Getting to know each other, weren't we, Nicki? (*He pauses*) Well, I have to be off; there's a crust to be made. Don't forget about tonight.
Liz Tonight?
Jack Dammit, you have forgotten. The Chamber of Commerce dinner. The main prize, Liz, keep your eye on the main prize. I'll be home early to get changed. Goodbye, Nicki, remember what I said. Leave you both to it, then.

Jack exits into the hallway

Liz "Remember what he said"? What did that mean?
Nicki He wants you to give up on me.
Liz Why would he want me to do that?
Nicki He says it's because you need a holiday.

A pause

Liz How are you feeling?
Nicki I slept through.
Liz Soon as I'm dressed I'll drive you home, but I need some coffee first.
Nicki Let me get it for you. I'd like to.
Liz Thank you.

Nicki exits into the kitchen

Liz remains still for a long moment, considering, then makes a decision, picks up the phone and punches out a number on it

Liz (*into the phone*) Harold. Liz Burns. I'm going to do you a favour, give
you a chance to demonstrate that new, government-funded computer. I
want readouts on Labrador House. ... OK, Harold, so you'll be doing me
a favour — would you just do it? ... Say, twenty years back and beyond.
Looking for a patient named Nicola White, aged about seven — birthday
December 25th. I want anything and everything, including staff attending,
every social worker who had contact with her. ... Of course I know it's
confidential! Everything we do is confidential. ... Thanks Harold — and
whatever you turn up, will you courier it over to me S.A.P.? Thanks. (*She
hangs up and thoughtfully picks up the teddy bear*)

*Nicki enters from the kitchen carrying a tray with a coffee pot, cups etc. on
it*

Nicki Da-da!
Liz It's nice to see you smile, you should do it more often.
Nicki Thank you.

*Liz takes the tray from Nicki and, during the following, pours cups of coffee
and drinks her own*

Liz What do you think of Jack?
Nicki He means well, I suppose — thinking of you.
Liz Does he — remind you of anyone?
Nicki Dunno. He seemed to think we might have met before.
Liz Have you?
Nicki Before yesterday? No, I don't think so. There is something about his
eyes, though ...
Liz Something familiar?
Nicki Calculating. Kind of eyes that, well ...
Liz That what?
Nicki Make you feel uncomfortable, as though he's undressing you. Mind
you, most men are like that.
Liz I'd better get ready.

Liz puts her coffee down and exits up the stairs

*Nicki stands and smiles at Liz until she has gone. The smile wipes away and
she looks grim and determined. She moves to the phone and makes to pick it
up. The phone rings under her hand. Nicki is startled and steps back for a
moment; then she picks up the phone*

Nicki (*into the phone*) Burns residence. ... Dr Pates? No I'm afraid she's not
here at the moment, nobody is except me. ... Nicola White. Nicki. I'm a

friend of the family. ... No, I'm not surprised you never heard of me. I've never heard of *you* either. ... (*She laughs, sharing a joke*) What? Your phone's been on the blink? ... No, I don't think she has been trying to reach you. ... Yes. ... Right, Dr Pates, I'll tell her you called. (*She hangs up, warily looks towards the stairs, then lifts the phone again and punches out a number. She pauses*) Billy, it's me. In half an hour the house will be empty and I've left a window at the back unlocked. Come in, do your work — what you do best — and then we'll screw the bastards.

CURTAIN

ACT II

The same. Later that night

The CURTAIN *rises on darkness. The answerphone light is blinking*

We hear the sound of a car arriving and stopping and the engine being switched off. A moment later we hear the front door open off stage

Jack (*off*) Whoops! What the devil is this?
Liz (*off*) What does it look like — a package.
Jack (*off*) Damned near fell arse over tit.

> *Jack and Liz enter from the hallway. Jack wears a dinner jacket and is not drunk but merry. He carries a bulky envelope. Liz wears a low-cut party frock and is stone cold sober*

They switch on the lights

(*Of the envelope*) It's addressed to you — delivered by hand, must be important.

Liz takes the envelope from Jack and puts it on the desk. She knows what it contains

Jack Ah. (*He pours a drink for each of them. Turning to hand one to Liz*) There we are.

Liz takes the drink from Jack. Jack pushes the drapes aside and looks out of the window

Liz I'm not sure I want one.
Jack Course you do, you deserve it — delegated driver's dues. Sorry it was your turn.
Liz It's always my turn.
Jack Well, it's no hardship for you, is it? At most you never have more than a couple of glasses of wine — not much to give up. You wouldn't have had time for even those tonight, your mouth was otherwise occupied, yakking on to Paul Stevens half the night. What were you talking about?

Liz I was asking him about Labrador House.

Jack Looked at one point as though you were interrogating him. His eyes got all glazed; poor old bugger would have fallen asleep if he hadn't had the occasional peep down your cleavage to buck him up!

Liz At least he only peeped.

Jack What does that mean?

Liz You weren't exactly restrained. The girl in the mini-dress.

Jack Her husband is influential, got lots of push.

Liz Not in the pelvic area, judging by the way she was thrusting her lower regions at you.

Jack We were only dancing.

Liz What do you call it, the groin to groin?

Jack Hey! You were jealous.

Liz Embarrassed.

Jack I was thinking of the coming election.

Liz I bet you were!

Jack Morton told me to put myself about, get to know people; if — when — I run as candidate I need them to remember me.

Liz She'll remember you all right, if only from the bruises.

Jack Dammit, you were jealous.

Liz You looked a fool, and her even more so; she was much too old to be wearing something as short as that.

Jack (*looking out of the window again*) You think that was short, you should see what the kids are wearing these days. I was at St Mary's School today, and I tell you, a fraction of an inch more and I could have got arrested for what I was thinking.

Liz Is that why you were at the school, to ogle the children?

Jack I wasn't at the school, I was just passing.

Liz You saw a hell of a lot "just passing".

Jack I was held up by a large woman carrying an even larger lollipop. (*He embraces Liz*) What's the matter, Liz, feeling your age? You don't have to … When I hold you close like this, the way you feel to me you're not a moment older than ——

Liz (*interjecting*) Seven years old?

Jack That'd be pushing it. If you were I would be arrested. I was going to say — no older than that first time I met you. Remember? You were lost, stopped to ask directions?

Liz You were outside a school that day too.

Jack Was I?

Liz What were you doing there?

Jack For God's sake, it was a long time ago. (*He regards her*) You've found out, haven't you?

Liz Found out what?

Jack Who was it, did Patsy blab?

Liz I haven't spoken to Patsy in weeks.

Jack Paul then, it was Paul.

Liz What have I found out?

Jack Come on, you know. My new assistant. She starts next week.

Liz What about her?

Jack She's a looker. My pimply office boy would say she is "fit". Tall, slim, legs up to her smile. (*He adds quickly*) I didn't choose her. She was sent down from Head Office. Patsy's been ribbing me about her, I think "male menopause" was mentioned on more than one occasion, but you don't have to worry, Liz — wherever her legs may end it's you I love — I'll always love.

Liz (*regarding Jack and shaking her head*) Still Jack the Lad.

Jack You've never called me that before. In fact, I don't think anyone's called me that since I was a student. Jack the Lad.

Liz Did you live up to it?

Jack (*taking another look out of the window*) That's for me to know and you to wonder about.

Liz What are you doing?

Jack Looking out of the window.

Liz I know that. And you keep doing it. Why? Are you expecting someone? Did you make an assignation with Miss Rub-Along? Or is your new assistant making a house call?

Jack If you must know, I thought someone was following us.

Liz You're not serious?

Jack No, really. From the moment we left the hotel there was a car behind us all the way. Didn't you notice it?

Liz There were lots of cars behind us.

Jack This one was different — had a broken headlight. It didn't stay behind us all the time, nothing as obvious as that, but it was there.

Liz Why on earth would anyone follow us?

Jack I dunno. (*Mock-serious*) Something from our past maybe. You put a knife-wielding maniac back on the streets, or I denied some layabout benefit. Dammit, there it is again. End of the close — one duff headlight.

Liz Where?

Jack Gonna find out what they think they're up to.

Liz Jack.

Jack exits into the hallway

Liz takes up a position looking out of the window, puzzled

There is a pause

Jack enters from the hallway

Liz I can't see any car.

Jack It's gone now, hasn't it? Must have seen me coming.

Liz You've had one too many.

Jack It was there.

Liz If you say so.

Jack Don't patronize me, Liz. There was a car, and I saw it — and no, I haven't had one too many ... More "one not quite enough". (*He picks up his drink and drains it. He pours another during the following*) Nectar from the gods. An oasis in the desert.

Liz What's bothering you?

Jack Nothing. Why do you ask?

Liz When you drink like this — there's usually something.

Jack Drinking like what? I'm merely bringing sustenance to a parched throat.

Liz You sound as though you're becoming dependent on the stuff ...

Jack This isn't stuff ... Pure malt Scotch.

Liz The needle to the addict.

Jack I'm not addicted. Put it down to my Scottish blood.

Liz You don't have an ounce of Scots in you.

Jack (*draining his glass and grinning*) I do now. (*He moves to again peer out from behind the drapes at the window*)

Liz It's gone. You said it was gone. If it ever existed.

Jack Why were you bending Paul's ear about Labrador House, eh? What's this obsession with Labrador House?

Liz It's not an obsession, it's — germane to a case I'm involved with.

Jack "Germane"? Now there's a word you don't encounter much outside of a crossword. "Germane". Seven letters meaning relevant or pertinent to. Pertinent to what? Labrador House? Or to that damned Nicki White who's been bugging you?

Liz You tell me. Was she ever at Labrador House?

Jack I'm sure you asked Paul the same question. After all, he was the Principal, he would know. Well, was she?

Liz He didn't remember. What about you? Do you remember her being there — a young and pretty seven-year-old — scared and ready for the taking?

Jack The taking! What the hell are you talking about?

Liz Do you remember her?

Jack No, I do not! And I would because I'm good with names. There were some Nicolas — but never a Nicki White. Liz, we both really need that holiday.

Liz regards Jack

And right now, a drink.

Liz You've had enough.

Jack I've had two — and three is my ambition. (*He moves to the drinks*) And you could do with another one to untighten whatever it is that's screwing you up. (*He pours drinks; as he does so, he notices the blinking light on the answerphone*) Got a message. Probably Janey. (*He presses the button and carries the two drinks over to Liz*)

Morton's Voice (*amplified; an older, Scots-tinged voice*) Jack. It's Ian Morton. I just caught the late news, I don't know if you have. Martha Myers is dead. Killed by a hit-and-run driver. Tragic. Not that I ever knew her. But you did, didn't you, Jack? You worked with her? I don't know how close you were, but there is bound to be some media interest — perhaps even a memorial service. It would be a fine opportunity for you to be seen and heard in sympathetic circumstances. Wouldn't do you any harm. Or the Party either. Call me tomorrow. (*The message snaps off*)

Morton's words hang in the air

Liz and Jack are very still. Finally Jack "breaks" and is impelled to go to the window, pull the drapes aside and look out

Liz What are you thinking?

Jack I don't know. I don't know what I'm thinking. Nobody there. (*He lets the drapes drop back into place*) Is this some kind of visitation? You start digging into Labrador House — and suddenly Martha is dead and we are at each other's throats … / what is going on …?

Liz (*interjecting*) Visitation? Something psychic, you mean? The Devil's work?

Jack (*pointing a finger at Liz*) You are becoming seriously weird.

Liz What was Martha Myers like?

Jack We've been through all this.

Liz I mean physically. Was she a large lady? Fat, ugly — like blubber? Would that describe her?

Jack I have to go to the loo.

Jack exits into the kitchen

Liz pauses, then prowls round the room to her desk and picks up the bulky envelope. She weighs it, hesitates, then tears it open to reveal various papers which she scans through. One particular section takes her attention. She begins to read it

Jack enters from the kitchen

And another thing. This Nicki White, who is she? What right does she have to come in and / disrupt this house ...?

Liz She's Nicola Craven. (*She consults the papers*) Born December 25th, Orkney. Taken to Labrador House on the morning of February 9th at 00.11 hours. That's just after midnight. Craven. White was her mother's name. Do you know her now?

Jack looks as though he has been hit

Jack Nicki Craven. Yes, I remember her — pretty little thing.

Liz I'm glad you admit it, because it says here that you were her case officer. Means you were in charge of her welfare. She was in your tender care. Well?

Jack Well, what? I don't know where this is going, or even what it's all about. Yes, a Nicki Craven was in my care. Admit it? Of course I admit it.

Liz You'd have to, it's a matter of record.

Jack If you would stop running around the houses and come to the point — any point ——

Liz Nicki was abused.

Jack That's why she was taken into care.

Liz Not before. After.

Jack What?

Crash! The sound of breaking glass upstairs

Liz and Jack move to gaze up the stairs

Liz What was that?

Jack Sounded like glass breaking.

Liz Perhaps the wind ...Did you leave a window open?

Jack Only the bathroom, no more than a couple of inches. Anyway, there's nothing to blow over up there.

They listen. The silence is acute

Liz Do you think there's someone in the house?

Jack Only one way to find out. (*He moves towards the stairs*)

Liz You're not going up there?

Jack Have you got a better idea?

Liz Phone the police.

Jack And look a complete berk when they find it was just the cat knocked over a vase?

Liz We don't have a cat.

Jack You know what I mean. (*He mounts the first stair*)
Liz Take something — protection, a weapon.
Jack Sure, just pass me your trusty automatic and a full clip of ammo.

Liz looks really scared. Jack steps down and picks up a weighty tome of a book

If he comes at me, I'll throw the book at him! (*He calls up the stairs*) All
right, if there's anyone up there, I'm coming up ...!

Jack exits up the stairs with the book

*There is a pause. Then Liz, despite herself, pulls aside the drapes and looks
out of the window. Leaving the drapes open she returns to the foot of the stairs*

(*Off*) Goddammit! Bastards!

Jack enters down the stairs and tosses the book down again

Would you believe it? Bloody vandals. There's glass everywhere and a
damned great hole in the window. Somebody's been taking pot shots at us
with an air rifle.
Liz Why would someone do that?
Jack These days they don't need a reason. Thank God it's only a window,
not even worth making an insurance claim.
Liz You're sure there's no-one in the house?
Jack Liz, it came from outside. (*He peers out of the window*) No sign of
anyone. They're long gone by now, whoever they were.
Liz We should report it, call the police.
Jack I think we have more important things to do, don't you? These papers,
Special Delivery — details of me and Lab House and Nicki Craven. Why,
Liz, what's going on?
Liz Why don't you tell me?
Jack Tell you what? I'm tired of this talking in riddles; whatever it is you
have to say, for God's sake come right out and say it!

*Crash! The undraped front window, directly behind Jack, shatters, (or
"stars" with a bullet hole in it) and at the same time he cries out and stumbles
to his knees, clutching the back of his head*

Liz Ohmigod! (*She kneels beside Jack*) Jack!
Jack I'm bleeding. (*He shows Liz his hand, now red with blood*) I've been
shot.
Liz (*examining Jack*) It's not too deep.

Jack Whatever, it bloody hurts. I feel groggy.
Liz Hold on.

Liz exits into the kitchen

Jack sways to his feet and sits heavily at the desk; in doing so, he sweeps the papers off the desk and on to the floor

Liz enters from the kitchen clutching a wet cloth and a Savlon spray. She moves to Jack and wipes his wound. He winces and yelps

Hold still. (*She sprays Jack with Savlon*)
Jack Yow!
Liz Who would have done this?
Jack Some louts with an air rifle.

Liz moves towards the shattered window

Keep away from the window! Call the police. Go on!
Liz (*picking up the phone to dial out*) The phone's dead.
Jack Dead? It can't be dead. It was working perfectly a few minutes ago.
Liz It's dead now.
Jack Let me ... (*He starts towards the phone*)

Suddenly, all the Lights go out and the stage is plunged into total black-out

Liz Jack — Jack!
Jack I'm here.
Liz There's a torch in my desk.

Jack moves to the desk and collides with it

Jack Damn! Found the desk. Which bloody drawer?
Liz Let me. (*She opens a drawer, produces a torch and switches it on*)

The Lights come on again. Jack and Liz regard each other, both getting really scared now

Jack It can happen, a hiccup in the powerlines. It's just a coincidence.

The Lights go out, plunging the room into total black-out. Pause

We hear a car drive up to the house and stop. A Light hits the shattered window and holds there, providing enough light to illuminate Jack and Liz

Liz (*warily moving closer to look out of the window*) A car. With one
   headlight.

*We hear the car rev and speed away; the light moves away and fades. The
stage remains in black-out for a long moment, then suddenly all the Lights
come on again*

Liz They're toying with us. Someone's trying to scare us.
Jack Someone's doing a helluva job! (*He is now galvanized into action,
   snatching up the phone, rattling at it, trying to restore it to life. Finally he
   gives up and turns to Liz*) Where's your mobile?
Liz I — I left it in the car.

Jack nods grimly and moves towards the hallway door

Liz You're not going out there?
Jack What else are we going to do? Sit here and wait for their next move?
   I'll only take a few seconds. (*He peers warily out of the window*) There's
   no sign of anyone now. (*He opens the hallway door*) I'll be in and out of
   the car as though a bear were snapping at my arse. I promise you.

   Jack exits quickly into the hallway

*Liz waits and frets. She sees the papers Jack spilled off the desk and is
compelled to pick them up. She moves to put them back on the desk, but scans
them instead*

Thump! There is a small sound from upstairs

Liz (*turning towards the stairs*) Hallo? Who's there? If there's someone up
   there, damned well show yourself!

Slam! The front door into the hallway, off, has slammed open

Jack (*off*) Liz!

   *The door from the hall slams open. Jack stands in the doorway, holding
   Liz's mobile phone aloft for the briefest moment*

Found it!

*Billy appears, startlingly, behind Jack. He is in his mid-twenties, and is
every middle-class, middle-aged person's nightmare, a painted punk, with
a shaved or dyed wild hairdo, jeans, torn T-shirt, heavy "bovver" boots,*

tattoos, face jewellery, and all the arrogance and angst of his kind. He carries a machete

Billy thrusts Jack forward with the point of the machete

(*Stumbling and falling into the room*) Ah ... ah ... ! (*He ends up lying on the floor*)

Billy grins and enters from the hallway, kicking the door closed behind him. He menacingly tosses the machete from hand to hand

Liz is frozen for a moment, then darts forward to snatch up the mobile phone — but instantly Billy has the machete at her breast or throat. She freezes. Billy grins and holds out his hand. Liz gives him the phone and he pockets it. Billy persists, moving her back with the machete. Jack tries to get to his feet; Billy moves like lightning with the machete, slashing at him. Jack yells and clutches his hand. He stays on his knees during the following

Liz Stop it! Just tell us what you want!
Nicki (*from upstairs; off*) That's better.

Nicki enters at the top of the stairs. Her clothes are brighter, wilder and sexier than before and she carries a sawn-off shotgun, levelled at the others

Nicki (*slowly descending the stairs*) Don't scream, Liz. There's nothing to scream about. Not yet. This is only the beginning.
Liz I wasn't going to scream.
Nicki In charge of yourself, are you? In charge of the situation? In a pig's eye!

Nicki suddenly moves very fast, shoving Liz with the gun and hustling her over to sit in a chair

Over there ... over there ... (*She swings back on Jack*) You stay where you are and keep your trap shut.
Liz He's hurt.
Nicki The poor little dear.

Liz controls her emotions, keeping her voice and attitude firm, trying to reassert some authority

Liz At least let him sit. I'm asking you, Nicki. Nicola.
Nicki (*after a hesitation*) Why not. (*She nods to Billy*)

Billy grabs Jack by the scruff of his neck and, demonstrating his strength, drags him to the sofa and dumps him on it

Liz (*encouraged, thinking she has won a point*) Why are you doing this?
Nicki I kept asking that. Why? Why are you doing this?
Liz You've been wronged, but this is no solution. You're a sick girl, Nicki.
Nicki (*with a smile*) Am I?
Liz It's not your fault, and I can help make you well again. Will you let me help you? Why don't you sit down, relax, and we'll talk it through. Like the last time. You felt better then, didn't you? With someone to listen — to understand?

Nicki moves Jack and gazes down on him, pointing the shotgun at him

Nicki Do you think he understands?
Jack If I knew what you were talking about ——

Nicki shoves the gun into Jack, silencing him

Nicki I told you to keep your trap shut.
Liz Do you know what time it is, Nicki? It's late. It'll be midnight soon.
Nicki (*turning to look at Liz*) Midnight. (*A beat, then a change of tack*) This is my brother, Billy. All the family I've got left. Smile nicely, Billy.

Billy smiles "nicely". It is quite chilling

Are you hungry, Billy?

Billy nods eagerly

The kitchen is through there. Go and take whatever you want.

Billy nods and turns to go, then hesitates

Don't worry, I've got this. (*She hefts the shotgun*)

Billy exits into the kitchen

He's younger than me so I have to take care of him now. Billy wasn't always like that — he was never bright, but he was talkative. Nineteen to the dozen. Then he changed. I expect it was some childhood experience. That's the phrase you shrinks like to fall back on, isn't it? Some bad, bad thing, back in the distant past.

Liz Nicki...

Nicki (*overriding*) Why am I doing this? For my own good — so I suppose it must be for your own good too. To lighten the darkness; not bright, dark, bright, dark, but all bright, light flooding in — into all those dark, nasty corners. Right, Jack? There's no cellar here, is there?

Jack (*baffled*) No.

Nicki I'll start in the attic then.

Jack Start what?

Nicki My search.

Billy enters from the kitchen, carrying a large plate heaped with food (including a green apple) and a bottle of beer

Nicki Got what you need, Billy?

Billy nods and sits down on the lowest of the stairs. He swigs his beer and tucks in during the following, eating with his fingers. He looks like Primeval Man

Liz What do you think you'll find in the attic?

Nicki The evidence. If not there it'll be somewhere in the house, tucked away in a cupboard, under a floorboard ... No matter where, I'll find it. I intend to be very thorough.

Liz What kind of evidence?

Nicki The porn. His kind always keep kiddy porn, don't they? Photos, tapes ...

Jack My kind! What do you mean — my kind?

Nicki (*to Liz*) I think you should tell him, don't you? Be better coming from you.

During the following line, Nicki points the gun at Jack, inches from his face

Jack If you're accusing me of ... (*He stops dead*)

Nicki I'm going to search the house from top to bottom, turn it over, trash the place if necessary. (*To Jack*) You know all about that, don't you? Keep searching until you find something — anything — and, my God, if I find one girlie magazine you are — damned! (*A beat. Her mood softens a bit*) I'm going to leave you now for a while. With Billy. Billy's very strong, aren't you, Billy? Show them how strong you are.

Billy grins, picks up the green apple, and crushes it in his fist

Nicki You might be silly enough to try and jump him, and, who knows, you might even succeed. But you're not going to try — even if Billy lay down, fell asleep, you wouldn't try. I'll show you why. (*She moves to the phone*) Come here, Liz. I want you to make a call.

Liz It isn't working.

Nicki (*lifting the phone and pressing the button*) It is now. Come here.

Liz moves to Nicki, who hands her the phone

Call your daughter.

Liz stares at her

Forgotten the number? It's 402954, but I want you to make the call. Go ahead!

Liz dials the number. Nicki punches the amplifier button

Let's all hear.

We hear the phone ringing out. A moment

Clancy's Voice Yeah?

Nicki Clancy, it's Nicki — is everything OK?

Clancy's Voice Yeah, this cottage is snug — got my vodka, TV, and the woman and kid under control.

Liz (*in a breath*) Janey.

This is the beginning of the ultimate horror for Liz and Jack

Nicki You know the drill?

Clancy's Voice Sure.

Nicki Repeat it for me, I want them to hear it.

Clancy's Voice OK. If I don't hear from you by midnight I go to work.

Liz No!

Nicki pushes Liz back and away

Nicki Make a note of the time, Clancy.

Clancy's Voice Got you. And Nicki ...? I'm sort of hoping you won't make that call.

Nicki Be in touch.

Liz No — please. (*She grabs the phone*)

The line buzzes. Clancy has hung up. Nicki takes the phone from Liz and hangs it up

Liz Janey and Molly ...

Jack You can't do this.

Nicki We can. And we will if we have to.

Liz Please — for pity's sake / don't do this ...

Nicki (*interjecting*) You keep using my words — "why" — "for pity's sake"... Tell her, Jack. They're water off a duck's back, aren't they? No sense in crying or pleading — it won't alter what has to be in the name of ... Well, what was it in the name of for you, Jack? The rules? The guidelines?

Jack I don't know why, but you think I've harmed you in some way. I haven't! But even if I had, don't take it out on her.

Nicki I'm educating her.

Jack Educating? What the / hell does that mean?

Liz We'll give you money — anything.

Nicki Shut up. Shut up both of you!

Pause. During the following Nicki hands the sawn-off shotgun to Billy, who props it by the stairs so he can continue eating

That's better. Let me spell it out: your daughter Janey, and your grand-daughter Molly, are in care. Clancy's care. Clancy is a short fuse, he's psychopathic. (*To Liz*) That's a condition you understand. I can control him — just. But have no doubt, if he doesn't hear from me by midnight he'll do it. Janey, Molly — the unborn baby. He won't do it because I told him — but because he likes to do it. I'm leaving you now for a while, so be good, won't you? Be very, very, good.

Jack You're monsters — monsters!

Nicki If we are, we're your creation.

Nicki exits up the stairs

The anguish and horror in Liz and Jack is almost tangible. During the following, Billy sits on the lower stair, eating happily, but pauses from time to time to take in what is being said and react to it. Liz and Jack are aware of his presence, of course, but are not sure just how much he is taking in

Jack Liz.

Liz Janey and Molly ...

Jack Liz, pull yourself together. We have to think. (*He looks at Billy*) Billy, do you understand what your sister has got you into? You won't get away with it, and you'll go to jail. Perhaps forever. Is that what you want, Billy? (*Encouraged, he stands up*) But that doesn't have to happen. We could speak on your behalf. Let me make one phone call…

Liz What are you thinking of? They have Janey and Molly — if she doesn't call / they'll kill them …

Jack (*interjecting*) If I call the police they should be able to get to the cottage in time.

Liz What if they don't?

They have temporarily forgotten Billy — but now he finishes his beer, belches happily, grins at Liz and Jack, demonstrates the empty bottle and exits into the kitchen to get some more, leaving the shotgun behind

Jack rushes to the phone and picks it up

Liz (*intervening*) No.

Jack (*listening to the phone*) It's dead again.

Liz (*panicking*) How will she make that call?

Jack He's got the mobile, hasn't he? (*He regards the closed kitchen door*) I'll wake 'em up next door. (*He hurries towards the hallway door*)

Liz (*panic rising*) No, Jack. (*She looks around frantically, sees the sawn-off shotgun by the stairs and grabs it up*) You go through that door, and I'll use it. I promise you, I'll use it. You're gambling with their lives — Janey and Molly.

Jack You'd shoot me? Point the damned thing there, (*he indicates the kitchen door*) point it at them.

Liz This was your doing.

Jack My doing? You brought her into this house — fed her dementia.

Liz Move away from the door. Move!

Jack moves away from the door

Jack Would you really shoot me, Liz, would you? Her craziness must be contagious.

Liz You brought us to this. You, Martha Myers — Labrador House.

Jack For Christ's sake, say something that makes sense to me.

Liz All right: Nicki White was at Labrador House.

Jack We've already been through that.

Liz She was seven years old, in your care, depending on you, trusting — and you betrayed that trust.

Jack How?

Liz You took her — abused her.

Jack (*seemingly stunned*) She told you that? She's lying — lying / through her teeth …

Liz (*interjecting*) No, she didn't tell me that. Her subconscious did, and that
   never lies.

Jack Did her "subconscious" come up with any proof — hard evidence?

Liz It's circumstantial.

Jack Indulge me.

Billy enters from the kitchen with a new bottle of beer

Jack and Liz barely notice Billy

*Billy pauses, listening. He swigs his beer then sits on the stairs again to watch
and listen, like someone watching a sideshow*

Liz The time, the place, Labrador House — you were there.

Jack A lot of people were there.

Liz With goatee beards? She described you.

Jack I told you, a lot of people had beards — even some of the women!

Liz And garlic on their breath?

Jack We were poorly paid, we lived on chilli con carne.

Liz And tobacco. The stale smell of tobacco?

Jack Is that it? The sum total of the evidence you'd convict me on?

Liz The man who attacked Nicki was called Jack. Jack the Lad.

Jack stares at Liz, stunned for a moment

Jack Liz. Darling. This is ridiculous, you can't even begin to believe that I
   would / abuse a child?

Liz (*overriding*) Janey and Molly are suffering now because of you and your
   disgusting lusts … You brought this upon us. God damn you, you are the
   Devil! (*She lifts the gun and aims it at Jack. Her finger tightens on the
   trigger*)

*Jack is frozen, horrified that Liz is going to pull the trigger. Billy gets to his
feet, eager to see what happens. Ultimately, Liz can't do it*

   *During the following, Nicki enters at the top of the stairs, carrying an
   envelope*

I can't.

Liz lowers the gun, distraught to the point of tears

Nicki Billy. Take the gun from her.

Billy tugs the gun from Liz's hands and leans it near the stairs

Nicki continues down the stairs and into the living-room

Jack You mad cow, you've brainwashed her with your own insane delusions!

Nicki Brainwashed is rich, coming from you. (*To Liz*) Is that what I've done, Liz, or have you reached your own conclusions about him? (*To Jack*) I said I'd educate her. Well, Liz? Do you still doubt my story?

Liz looks from Nicki to Jack

Liz All those years sharing his bed, having his baby … Surely I would have detected something? I'm trained to do that.

Nicki They're clever — crafty — it's part of their disease, hiding things. But "seek and ye shall find". (*She proffers the envelope*) Tucked away at the back of his bedside table. (*To Jack*) So you could lie in bed, look at them, and imagine.

Liz What are they?

Nicki Photos.

Liz looks accusingly at Jack

Jack Liz, I promise you — I've no idea.

Nicki Let's look at them, shall we? Examine them for their implications. (*She takes a photo out of the envelope*) Exhibit A. A small child, scantily clad, sitting on his knee.

Jack That's Janey. (*To Liz*) You remember — her third birthday … ?

Nicki On his knee. Exhibit B. (*A second photo*) It gets worse. The same small child naked — and he is watching her.

Jack That's on the beach in Marbella.

Nicki But look at his eyes — watching her, lusting after her …

Liz He's her father.

Jack That's right, for godssakes — I'm loving her.

Nicki You see, he admits it.

Jack That isn't what I meant, and you damned well know it … Can't a father look at his own daughter?

Nicki With that carnal look in his eyes?

Jack That's a matter of interpretation

Nicki Exactly. Exhibit C, this is the clincher. (*A third photo*) It's hands-on. A child of no more than eighteen months. A baby, stark naked — and he's touching her.

Jack I was bathing Molly.

Nicki Bathing? Can we be sure of that? Look at your hands. Touching and fondling her.

Jack You can't see my hands, they're deep in the bubbles, you can't see what I'm doing! (*He stops, realizing what he has said*) Liz, you took that picture — do you remember?

Liz I remember you insisting that I take it.

Jack Are you going mad, or am I? Do you really believe I could be capable of abusing Janey or Molly? I love them both dearly. I wouldn't harm them. I couldn't.

Liz Please make that call. You've convinced me; I have no doubts now, you've got what you wanted, haven't you? What you came here for?

Nicki just stares at Liz

Look, I'll support you; no matter how long ago it was, we'll make a case against him, see that he gets what he deserves for what he did to you. I'm begging you to make that call.

Nicki Do you think that's all this is about? Oh, yes, I want my revenge, retribution — but not for me. Not just for me. You don't know the half of it — what he's capable of. He's a killer too. He murdered my father!

CURTAIN

SCENE 2

The same. The action is continuous

Nicki Yes, he murdered my father. Stuck a knife through his heart.

Jack Can't you see now she's quite mad?

Liz I don't believe that. He isn't capable of that.

Nicki A little while ago you didn't think him capable of child abuse. I've never told you the details of that, have I? Of what he did to me? The gory details?

Liz I think I can imagine.

Nicki Do you like to pull the wings off flies? No, you can't imagine.

Liz Make the call. Please.

Nicki (*overriding*) I want you to know what he did to me — I need you to understand ...

Jack lunges for the shotgun leaning against the stairs, but Billy is quicker; he gets there first, grabs the gun and shoves Jack away with it — hard — sending him falling, stumbling back to end up in a heap on the sofa

Nicki See how desperate he is to keep the truth from you?
Jack Liz …
Liz Shut up!

Liz looms over Jack

Shut your mouth, don't say another word. (*To Nicki*) I'll hear you out, but you must promise me you'll make that call.
Nicki You're in no position to dictate terms.
Liz I'm not the guilty party here, neither are Janey or Molly. I took you in, Nicki, I tried to help you …
Nicki (*interjecting*) It was Friday night. I know because we were excited that Dad was going to take us to the zoo the next day. Remember that, Billy? The zoo, and after — an ice cream, and maybe even the pictures. Dad put us to bed like he always did. First Billy in his room, me in mine. I was so excited Dad had to sit with me for a while calming me. He tucked me in. Gave me my teddy bear to cuddle. Uncle Ted. He kissed me. He always kissed me, called me his little pudding. I don't know what woke me: the smashing of the door? The sound of the church clock chiming twelve midnight? Or him? Bending over me, lifting me from my bed. I could hear Billy screaming in the next room. He carried me down the stairs. I could hear my dad then — shouting, fighting, and men, I suppose they must have been cops, restraining him. Hurting him. He called to me, and I wanted to call back, to say, "Daddy, I love you", but he wouldn't let me. Covered my mouth. Took me to the car, with just a blanket over my jim-jams — and my knickers. Dad always made me wear knickers in case I had an — accident. I did then. I wet them. They put me in a car, took me away. I kept saying I wanted my daddy — I wanted Uncle Ted. They wouldn't let me have either: my dad because he was suspect — the perpetrator — and Uncle Ted because he might be a symbol — can you imagine that? They thought my teddy bear might be a trigger for something evil — for satanic rites? My teddy bear. They — he— took me to Labrador House. Not with Billy though! They took him somewhere else — in case we colluded. I didn't see Billy again for more'n four months. I missed him. I missed Billy, and my dad, and Uncle Ted. I cried for them, but they didn't take any notice. They undressed me. It was so cold there. Then they brought in that woman — Martha Myers. She was fat and ugly. Him and her. They kept asking me questions, over and over, then they weren't questions any more, they were suggestions: did your father do this? Did he do that? Awful things I'd never heard of before, things that made me feel sick — things I didn't understand. I kept telling them my dad was good, he was loving — but that wasn't what they wanted to hear. They had the evidence by then; they'd trashed the house and found the photos: me, my dad and Billy, by the sea — and, oh

my God, in some of those photos Billy and me were nearly naked — we were in bathing suits! And there were the other ones Dad had taken when we were just tiny kids — in the bath. And worst of all, during the search they'd turned up a tatty, moth-eaten copy of *Playboy*. I'm not even sure it was my dad's — could have been left over from the last tenant — but that was enough for him and her. Dad was tried and convicted — but none of this ever took place in a court of law. He was guilty in their eyes — in their opinion. They kept on at me more now. So I started to tell them what they wanted to know, particularly that fat bitch! I told them that what they had suggested, what they had put into my mind, actually happened. Like when you took me back, Liz. Did you really think I was fooled by that hypnotic crap? Did you like my performance? I was wide awake the whole time, and going along with whatever you wanted. It was the same with them. I got tired. I gave them what they wanted, I gave them what their twisted and evil minds had put into mine. I made up stories I knew would please them. (*She puts her head in her hands, unable to go on for a while*)

Liz Oh, sweet Jesus. (*She moves to Nicki*) Nicki.

Jack Did you hear what she said? I didn't touch her. I didn't abuse her.

Liz She was torn from her bed, frightened, bewildered, separated from her family — even her goddamned, bloody teddy bear! She was seven years old, Jack! Younger than Molly. What constitutes abuse to you?

Jack It was the / system ...

Liz (*interjecting*) If you say it was the system, I'll rip your heart out with my bare hands! Nicki ...

Nicki You didn't abuse my body, you abused my mind, my rights — my dignity. But you — killed him. My dear daddy. Murdered him. I'd like to tell you about my daddy...

Liz First make that call, Nicki. Please.

Nicki He was a fine man. After my mum died, he was always there for us. A loving man, I think he tried to make up for Mum being gone by loving us twice as much. He was always hugging us, kissing — loving.

Jack He was exonerated.

Liz I told you to shut up.

Billy affirms this by putting the machete close to Jack

Nicki Yes, it all ended eventually. Not "happily" — but certainly "for ever after". We finally had our day in court, and the judge saw things for what they were — bullshit! Martha Myers went back to America — discredited. But she still has her disciples.

Liz Martha Myers is dead.

A moment

Nicki Yes, I heard that. She was a disease, a cancer that could still spread. Her theories — born out of what? A hormonal disturbance? Her own childhood experiences? Spite? Anyway, her death has come far too late for my daddy. He was murdered long before. The French touch, Italians embrace. Even Russians kiss! My dad was a true European — he hugged and kissed whenever he could. But there was nothing behind it except, "I love you, I want to show that I love you". Yes, he was exonerated. But mud sticks. We moved house, he made us use our mother's name.

Jack I did not kill your father.

Nicki He was ashamed. There was no reason for him to be, but he was ashamed. There were still fingers pointing, tongues wagging — and you know what they say? No smoke without fire? People pulled their children off the streets when he walked by — can you imagine what that did to him? It changed him. It changed us. He didn't kiss me any more, if I went to hug him he would push me away — or he'd look behind him first. Like a guilty man. When you can't touch or be touched, love dries up. Yes, he still loved us, I knew that, but you put a barrier between us — a vacuum. You took the warmth of his love and turned it into an icy cold void. What we once had was lost forever. Do you know what I got in exchange? An inquiry, then an inquiry into the inquiry. Disclaimers from an authority who promised so much, but in the end did nothing at all. A freemasonry of the inept closed ranks to protect their own failings. Dad died three years later. They said cardiac arrest, but it wasn't. His poor, loving heart was broken. You did that. You killed him just as surely as if you'd stuck a knife in him. We've drifted since then, me and Billy. Billy took it even harder than me — you can see, he's different now. No, you can't see, you didn't know him before. He was — outgoing. Yes, he can hold down a job, but he doesn't trust anyone any more — he can't relate to anyone except me. We've been waiting a long while, Jack Burns, for the right time, the right opportunity — to arrange for you to think Pates was away — and pretend I was his patient, referred to you. That's why I'm here. Why I did this. Someone has to pay.

Liz Not my family. Make that call, Nicki.

Nicki regards Liz

It's nearly midnight.

Nicki It's after midnight. Didn't you know? Several minutes after midnight.

Liz God, please — call him, call him now!

Nicki You should know that Billy isn't bright, but he does have his talents. A dead shot with an air rifle — and a whiz with wires. (*She moves to the phone*) He broke in earlier and fixed your phone.

Jack He rigged it?

Nicki Same way he faked up Freddy Pates' answerphone — yes, he fixed this too ... No matter what number you punch out, it always connects with Clancy. He's a friend of ours with a taste for the dramatic. Sitting at home in his room now. Dreaming of Hollywood.

Liz My daughter?

Nicki At home asleep, I imagine. I don't even know where she lives — just her phone number. (*She punches a button on the phone*) Normal service is restored. You can call her if you want, but I don't think she'll be too pleased at this time of night. When you pointed that gun at him, your finger a whisker away from pulling the trigger, even though it's not loaded — I knew then I'd won.

Liz stares at her

Nicki We're hurt. The walking wounded. But we are not monsters. Billy.

Billy moves with Nicki towards the hallway door

Love shouldn't be penalized. Families should be able to embrace and kiss without fear. Tell them that. Spread the word — don't let this happen to someone else. That's all I ever wanted. (*She opens the door*)

Liz regards Nicki, then moves to her

Liz What about Martha Myers?

Unexpectedly it is Billy who replies

Billy (*in a "who you lookin' at" tone*) Yeah? What about her?

Nicki and Billy exit into the hallway on this ambiguous, chilling note

Liz and Jack are alone

CURTAIN

FURNITURE AND PROPERTY LIST

ACT I

SCENE 1

On stage: Sofa
Comfortable chairs
Standard lamp
Table or desk. *On it*: table lamp, framed photographs, desk diary, pens,
    papers and forms etc. *In drawer*: torch
Framed diploma
Radio
Drinks (including mineral water, whisky, brandy) and glasses
Books, including at least one weighty tome, bric-a-brac, high-tech
    phone (on shelves)

Off stage: Spatula (**Liz**)
Two squash racquets (**Jack**)

Personal: **Jack**: wrist-watch (worn throughout)

SCENE 2

Off stage: Full glass of wine (**Liz**)
Roughly wrapped package containing moth-eaten, battered teddy bear
    (**Nicki**)
Smallish chiming clock (**Liz**)

SCENE 3

Off stage: Tray with coffee pot and cups on it (**Nicki**)

ACT II

SCENE 1

Off stage: Bulky envelope (**Jack**)
Wet cloth and Savlon spray (**Liz**)

Mobile phone (**Jack**)
Machete (**Billy**)
Sawn-off shotgun (**Nicki**)
Large plate heaped with food including prop crushable apple; bottle of
    beer (**Billy**)
Second bottle of beer (**Billy**)
Envelope containing at least three photographs (**Nicki**)

Personal: **Jack**: blood capsule

SCENE 2

No additional props

LIGHTING PLOT

Practicals required: flashing light on answerphone, table lamp, standard lamp
One interior with exterior backing behind windows. The same throughout

ACT I, Scene 1

To open: General interior lighting with late summer afternoon effect on exterior
backing

No cues

ACT I, Scene 2

To open: General interior lighting with practical lamps on; night effect on exterior
backing

Cue 1	**Liz** turns some of the lights off	(Page 16)
	Cut some lights to leave sofa area lit	
Cue 2	**Liz** pushes button on answerphone	(Page 19)
	Answerphone light blinks (continuous)	
Cue 3	**Liz** restores the main lights	(Page 19)
	Restore lights to opening setting	
Cue 4	**Liz** switches on answerphone	(Page 21)
	Light stops blinking	

ACT I, Scene 3

To open: General interior lighting with practical lamps off; morning effect on exterior
backing

No cues

ACT II, Scene 1

To open: Darkness. Answerphone light blinks (continuous)

| *Cue* 5 | **Liz** and **Jack** switch on the lights | (Page 27) |
| | *Bring up general interior lights and lamps* | |

Cue 6	**Jack** presses the button on the answerphone *Cut answerphone light*	(Page 31)
Cue 7	**Jack** starts towards the phone *Black-out*	(Page 34)
Cue 8	**Liz** switches the torch on *Bring up full lighting*	(Page 34)
Cue 9	**Jack**: "It's just a coincidence." *Black-out*	(Page 34)
Cue 10	Sound of car driving up to house *Car light hits the window*	(Page 34)
Cue 11	Car revs and speeds away *Car light moves away and fades*	(Page 35)
Cue 12	Pause after fade of car light *Bring up full lighting*	(Page 35)

ACT II, SCENE 2

To open: As end of ACT II, SCENE 1

No cues

EFFECTS PLOT

ACT I

ACT II

Cue 13   **Jack**: "What?"   (Page 32)
             Sound of breaking glass from upstairs

Cue 14   **Jack**: " ... come right out and say it!"   (Page 33)
             Window shatters or "stars"

Cue 15   Black-out. Pause   (Page 34)
             Sound of car driving up to house

Cue 16   **Liz**: "A car. With one headlight."   (Page 35)
             Car revs and speeds away

Cue 17   **Liz** scans the papers   (Page 35)
             Small thumping sound from upstairs

Cue 18   **Liz**: " ... damned well show yourself!"   (Page 35)
             Front door slams open

Cue 19   **Nicki**: "Let's all hear."   (Page 39)
             Dialling tone over phone speaker; then dialogue as p.39

Cue 20   **Liz** grabs the phone   (Page 39)
             Line buzzes

www.ingramcontent.com/pod-product-compliance
Lightning Source LLC
LaVergne TN
LVHW051805080426
835511LV00019B/3413